Presents

DISCOVERING

Wind and Water

A collection of texts

to accompany

Steps to Discovering
Wind and Water

KARINA YOUNK

Art Image Publications

Thoughtsteps is an intermediate learning resource based on the integration of language arts, science, and social studies, along with other subject areas and processing skills, whenever there are natural links. *Thoughtsteps* can be used with the entire class, with small groups, with individual students, or as a learning centre.

EDITORS:

Catherine Stewart

Andrew Vandal

Maryse Bérubé

STUDENT EDITORS:

Shannon Provencher

Alexandre Fallon

STYLISTIC EDITING:

Joan Irving

PILOT CLASSES:

Cathie Eck, Grade 4/5

Quarterway Elementary, Nanaimo, B.C.

Katya Roy, Grade 7

Pauline Haarer Elementary, Nanaimo, B.C.

ISBN: 1-896876-05-6

CANADA

Art Image Publications Inc.

3281 Jean-Beraud Avenue

Laval, QC

H7T 2L2

Tel: (514) 334-5912

    1 800 361-4504

Fax: (514) 688-6269

U.S.A.

Art Image Publications Inc.

61 Main Street

P.O. Box 568

Champlain, N.Y. 12919

Tel: 1 800 361-2598

Fax: (518) 298-5433

Printed in Canada

Table of Contents

Between Earth and Sky

The Hot Air Balloon Festival

Let's Construct a Hot Air Balloon

On the way home from school, Alex spotted Dominique in an open field. Dominique was flying her kite and creating all kinds of patterns in the sky.

"Dominique, you sure know how to fly that kite! Have you been practising for a long time?"

"No, not long at all!" answered Dominique, still concentrating on the direction of the wind. "I only started this summer. We spent our holidays near the ocean. That's where my mom bought me this kite. On the beach, there was a kite festival with all kinds of wonderful kites. There were diamond-shaped kites like mine, but there were also box kites, dragon kites, and hang-gliders! One man had even attached seven diamond kites together with brightly coloured ribbons."

"Hey! I went to a festival, too!" exclaimed Alex. "But instead of flying kites, people were flying balloons."

"Balloons? What kind of balloons?" Dominique asked.

"Hot air balloons. You know," explained Alex, "the kind with a basket, called a nacelle, tied underneath that people can ride in. A big burner, attached under the opening of the balloon, heats the air inside the balloon and makes it fly."

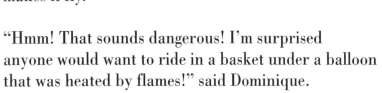

"Hmm! That sounds dangerous! I'm surprised anyone would want to ride in a basket under a balloon that was heated by flames!" said Dominique.

"Well, at the festival this summer, I learned that the hot air balloon was the first invention that enabled people to fly," Alex went on. "Hot air balloons were invented over two hundred years ago. Two brothers in France built the first one. Can you guess their names?"

"I have no idea!" replied Dominique.

"Their names were Joseph and Jacques-Étienne Montgolfier. That's why, in French, a hot air balloon is called a *Montgolfière*."

"That's fascinating!" Dominique answered, most impressed. "Hmm, I wonder which came first, kites or balloons?"

"I'm going home to find out!" exclaimed Alex, as he waved good-bye to Dominique. "See you tomorrow, Dominique!"

"Bye, Alex!"

As soon as Alex got home, he ran into his room and dropped onto his bed. Lying there, looking out of his window, Alex admired the clouds drifting by. They looked like great puffy white balloons.

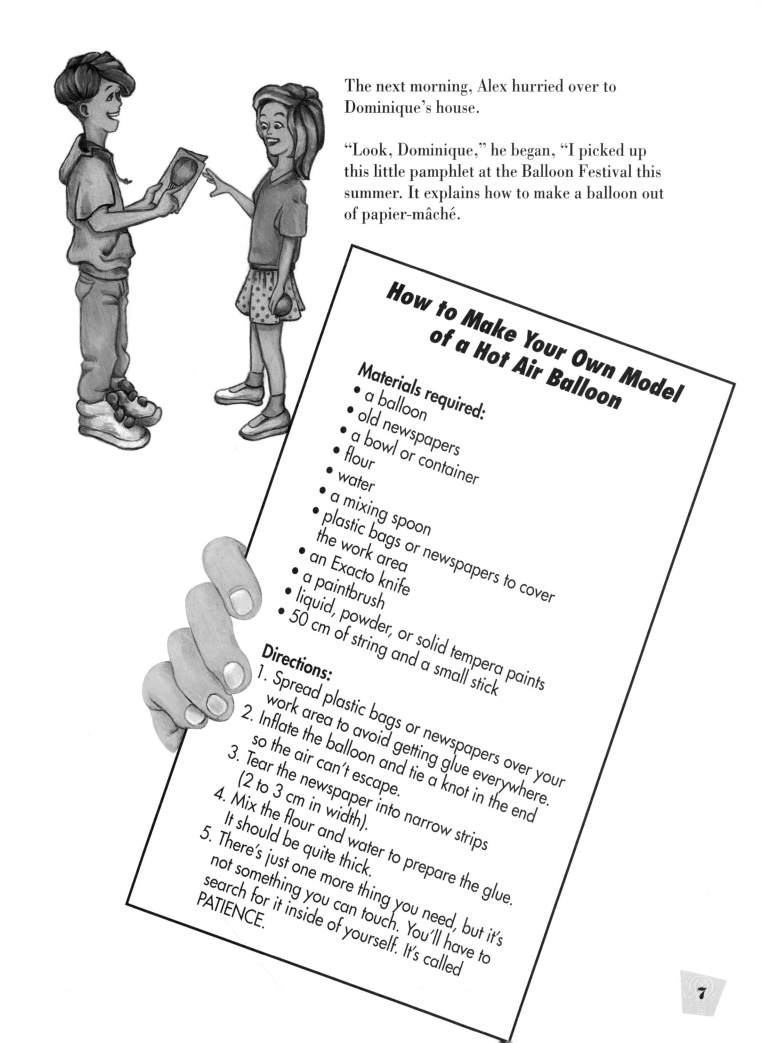

The next morning, Alex hurried over to Dominique's house.

"Look, Dominique," he began, "I picked up this little pamphlet at the Balloon Festival this summer. It explains how to make a balloon out of papier-mâché."

How to Make Your Own Model of a Hot Air Balloon

Materials required:
- a balloon
- old newspapers
- a bowl or container
- flour
- water
- a mixing spoon
- plastic bags or newspapers to cover the work area
- an Exacto knife
- a paintbrush
- liquid, powder, or solid tempera paints
- 50 cm of string and a small stick

Directions:
1. Spread plastic bags or newspapers over your work area to avoid getting glue everywhere.
2. Inflate the balloon and tie a knot in the end so the air can't escape.
3. Tear the newspaper into narrow strips (2 to 3 cm in width).
4. Mix the flour and water to prepare the glue. It should be quite thick.
5. There's just one more thing you need, but it's not something you can touch. You'll have to search for it inside of yourself. It's called PATIENCE.

Constructing the Balloon

1. Soak a strip of newspaper in the glue mixture.

2. Slide the strip through your fingers to get rid of the excess glue.

3. Lay the strip on the balloon, taking care to place it as flat as possible all around the balloon. The more careful you are, the better your hot air balloon will look when it's finished.

4. Continue to cover the entire surface of the balloon with strips. Try to cover the balloon with at least three layers so that the papier-mâché will be very solid when it dries.

5. Ask an adult to help you with this step. Let the balloon dry completely, then cut an opening in the base of the balloon. For this, you will need an Exacto knife. **Be extremely careful not to hurt yourself!** Look at the illustration below to see where to cut. At the same time, poke four small holes around the base of the balloon and one at the top. These will be for attaching the nacelle (basket) and for hanging the balloon.

6. Next apply a foundation or primer coat of white paint. Once the first coat is dry, decorate the balloon with the colours and designs of your choice.

7. While you're working on your basket (the nacelle), you might want to hang your balloon in a safe place. Thread the string through the hole in the top of the balloon. Attach the stick to the string inside the balloon to keep the string from slipping out.

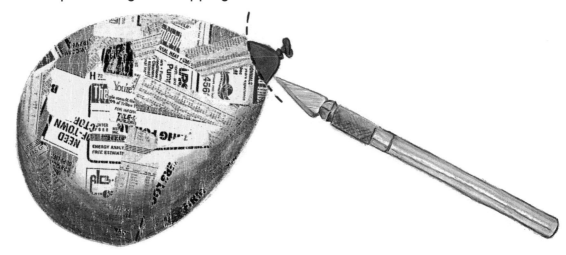

Constructing the Nacelle of the Balloon

Materials required :
- scissors
- glue
- a ruler
- graph paper
- construction paper
- scraps of coloured paper
- 4 strings, each 15 cm long

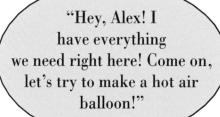

"Hey, Alex! I have everything we need right here! Come on, let's try to make a hot air balloon!"

Directions:

1. On a piece of graph paper make a pattern like this one:
   - Each side of the nacelle measures 5 cm x 5 cm, and there are six sides. (These are the faces of the cube.)
   - Each joining strip is 1 cm wide and 5 cm long. There are five in all.
   - The dotted lines indicate the folds that will form the edges of the nacelle.
   - The solid lines are the lines you will cut along.

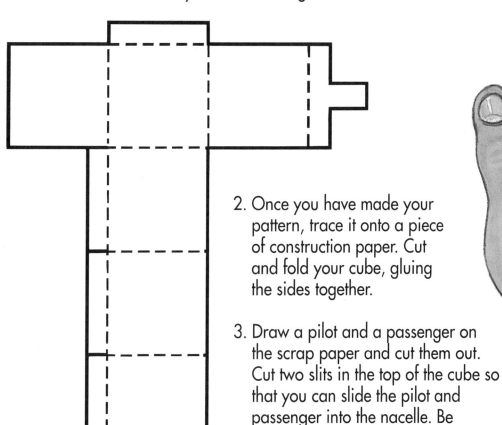

2. Once you have made your pattern, trace it onto a piece of construction paper. Cut and fold your cube, gluing the sides together.

3. Draw a pilot and a passenger on the scrap paper and cut them out. Cut two slits in the top of the cube so that you can slide the pilot and passenger into the nacelle. Be careful not to cut yourself!

4. Finish your nacelle by decorating the sides with scrap paper.

5. Tie the nacelle to the balloon by attaching the strings to each of the four sides of the nacelle and then to the four holes in the base of the balloon.

How Does It Fly?

Alex and Dominique stood admiring their hot air balloon.

"Oh, wouldn't it be wonderful if it could fly?" sighed Dominique.

"You know, the Montgolfier brothers had to do lots of experiments before they succeeded in making their balloon fly. At first, they thought that it was the smoke from the fire that would make the balloon rise."

Experiment No. 1: Does Air Expand and Contract?

Hypothesis: If air expands when it is heated, a balloon should inflate and deflate when the air temperature inside changes.

Materials required:
- two deep bowls or containers
- an empty bottle
- ice cubes
- a balloon
- a kettle

Directions:
1. Fill the first container with boiling water.
2. Fill the second container with cold water and ice.
3. Stretch the opening of the balloon over the neck of the bottle.
4. Slowly place the bottle in the container of hot water. Observe what happens to the balloon after two minutes.
5. Remove the bottle from the hot water. Wait until the balloon starts to deflate then put the bottle in the ice water. Observe what happens to the balloon.

Illustration:

a container of boiling water

a balloon

a kettle

an empty bottle

a container of ice water

Caution: Be careful near boiling water!

Observations: When the air inside the bottle is heated, the balloon expands. When the bottle is cooled, the balloon deflates and then is sucked inside the bottle.

Conclusion: When air is heated, it takes up more space (it *dilates* or *expands*). Air *contracts* or takes up less space when it is cooled.

Dominique interrupted, "No way! Everyone knows that it's the hot air that makes objects rise! Come and see how it works."

Experiment No. 2 : Abracadabra! Watch the Dancing Bags!

Hypothesis: If hot air takes up more space than cold air, then a container filled with hot air should weigh less than one of equal size filled with cold air.

Materials required:
- a metre-stick
- two large sheets of aluminum foil (about 30 cm x 30 cm)
- a string about 30 cm long
- two strings about 15 cm long
- a candle   • matches

Directions:
1. Form two bags by folding the sheets of aluminum foil as shown.
2. Suspend the metre-stick from the longest string so that it balances freely.
3. Using the shorter strings, suspend the two bags, one at each end of the metre-stick, so that their openings face downward.
4. Adjust the metre stick so that both sides are balanced.
5. Place a lit candle beneath one of the aluminum bags.
6. Observe what happens to the bags.

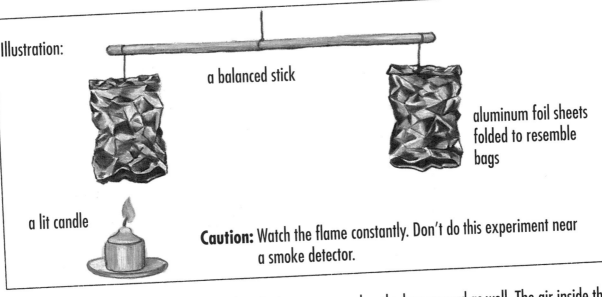

Illustration:

a balanced stick

aluminum foil sheets folded to resemble bags

a lit candle

Caution: Watch the flame constantly. Don't do this experiment near a smoke detector.

Observation: The heat of the flame makes the bag suspended above it rise.

Conclusion: The air heated by the candle expands and rises above the cooler, more dense air surrounding it. The heated air gets caught in the aluminum foil bag and pushes the bag upward as well. The air inside the bag expands and some escapes, making the heated bag lighter than the bag filled with cold air. Hot air balloons are able to rise because of the hot air they contain. As soon as the air inside starts to cool, the balloon begins its descent back to earth.

"Alex, my sister suggested two other experiments that we could try. I copied them down in my science notebook. Let's try them so that I can complete the observations and conclusions in my book.

Date: Saturday, September 30, 1997

by Dominique

Title: A Mini Hot Air Balloon

Hypothesis: I am going to try to imitate a hot air balloon by using a plastic dry-cleaning bag and a blow dryer. I think that the hot air will make the bag rise high into the sky!

Materials:
• plastic dry-cleaning bag or large garbage bag
• blow dryer

Directions:
1. Hold the bag over the blow dryer
2. Turn on the blow dryer.
3. Let go of the bag.

Illustration:

plastic bag,

blow dryer

Caution: Be careful not to let the blow dryer overheat. Never touch an electrical outlet with your hands.

Observations:

Conclusion:

Date: Saturday, September 30, 1997

Title: Heat and Wind   by Dominique

Hypothesis: I want to try to create wind currents by using a lamp. I think that if hot air
rises, it should move through the cooler air around it. Therefore, a paper spiral
held in the current should turn as the air moves.

Materials:
- an electric light or lamp
- a pencil with an eraser at the end
- a straight-pin
- a piece of aluminum foil
- scissors

Directions:
1. Using the scissors, cut a spiral out of the foil as shown below.
2. Stick the straight-pin into the eraser end of the pencil.
3. Balance the spiral on the end of the straight-pin. It might be necessary to make
   a slight indentation in the foil so that it will stay on.
4. Hold the pencil by its tip over the lamp.
5. Light the lamp and wait a few minutes for the surrounding air to heat up.

Illustration:

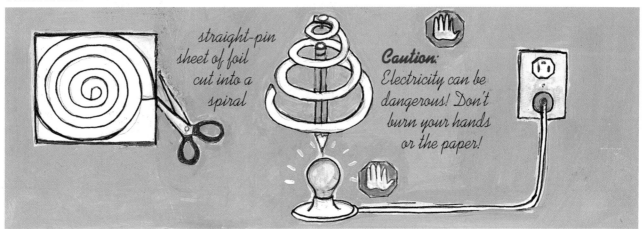

straight-pin
sheet of foil
cut into a
spiral

Caution:
Electricity can be
dangerous! Don't
burn your hands
or the paper!

Observations:

Conclusion:

Let's Organize a Festival

"Alex!" shouted Dominique, "I have an idea! We could organize a festival in our class."

"Are you sure? What kind of festival?" asked Alex.

"A hot air balloon festival, of course!" continued Dominique, all excited. "We could show everyone how to construct a hot air balloon and we could do a research project on the Montgolfier brothers and other pioneers of flight. With the experiments in my books, we could show how hot air makes some objects rise."

"What a fantastic idea!" exclaimed Alex. "Why, we could even invite other classes to come and take part in our festival."

"But how are we going to organize all that?"

A Page in History

The Success of the Montgolfier Brothers

People have wanted to fly since the beginning of time. An old Greek legend talks about a man named Icarus who tried to fly after gluing feathers to his arms and body. But it was not until 1783 that the Montgolfier brothers, from France, invented a vehicle that would enable people to really fly. Here is a description of their adventure.

While standing in his mother's kitchen, in Annonay, France, Joseph de Montgolfier watched the smoke rise over the cooking fire. He thought about it and asked himself, "If smoke rises from a fire, shouldn't it be possible to fill an object with smoke and make it rise?"

With the help of his brother, Jacques-Étienne, Joseph started experimenting by holding paper bags and, later, bags made of silk over very smoky fires. Luckily, they soon discovered that they needed hot air and not smoke to fill and lift their balloons.

On June 5, 1783, they succeeded in making a balloon filled with hot air rise 1 500 metres in the sky.

They completed their first "passenger" flight on September 19, 1783, at Versailles before King Louis XVI. In the nacelle attached beneath the huge balloon were three passengers: a rooster, a lamb, and a duck. This balloon travelled three kilometres and rose nearly 500 metres in the air! The animals landed safely with only one small accident. The lamb broke one of the rooster's wings in his hurry to get out!

Later, a young historian by the name of Pilâtre de Rozier offered to be the first man to fly in the balloon.

For the first attempt, the balloon was attached to the ground by heavy ropes, and Pilâtre de Rozier had a great time making the balloon bob up and down.

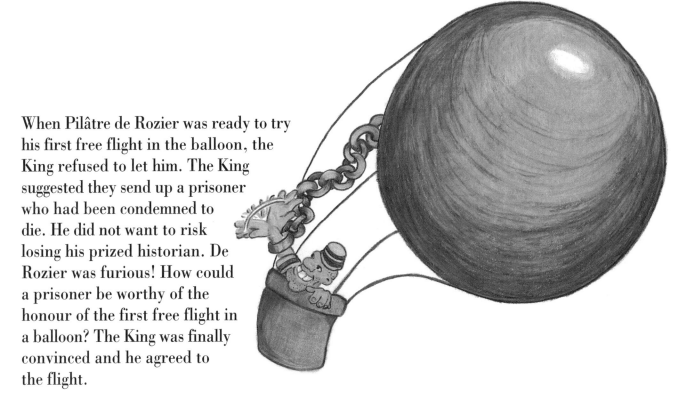

When Pilâtre de Rozier was ready to try his first free flight in the balloon, the King refused to let him. The King suggested they send up a prisoner who had been condemned to die. He did not want to risk losing his prized historian. De Rozier was furious! How could a prisoner be worthy of the honour of the first free flight in a balloon? The King was finally convinced and he agreed to the flight.

So, at 2:00 p.m. on November 21, 1783, Pilâtre de Rozier and his good friend, the Marquis of Arlandes, took off in the balloon named The Globe. The balloon was 15 metres in diameter and 22 metres high. Their flight began at the Château de la Muette, near Paris. There were a few problems during the flight. First, the flame burned small holes in the balloon. Then, the fabric started to tear at the seams. Finally, the two travellers very nearly crashed into the belltower of a church! But at last, after 25 minutes in the air, the pair landed safely eight kilometres from where they had started their flight.

The age of aeronautics took off quickly after this. Only ten days later, Dr. Charles, a professor at the French Academy, succeeded in another feat. He flew in a balloon filled with hydrogen. His flight lasted almost two hours, and he travelled a distance of 44 kilometres. Nothing could stop the pioneers of flight now!

My Game's a Washout!

My Baseball Game's a Washout!

Hi there! I'm 12. My name's Ben and I love baseball. That's all you need to know about me. The rest is unimportant. School, computers, and television are for killing time whenever I'm not playing baseball. Baseball is all that counts. Baseball is the reason I get up early on Saturday mornings. The posters that cover the walls and ceiling of my bedroom are of pitchers, batters, and back-catchers! I even have a poster of a gold baseball bouncing off of a silver bat and landing in a bronze baseball mitt. Stamp, rock, and coin collections – they're for other people. Me? I collect baseball cards!

Frank, one of my friends, just called. He wants to cancel our practice session so he can go swimming. Can you imagine choosing a swim in the lake over a baseball practice? That's it! Frank is no longer my friend. Anyone with that kind of attitude is no longer a member of my gang. I'll call Patrick instead.

"Patrick! Do you want to come and hit a few fly balls at the park?
–…
Great! I'll meet you there in 10 minutes.
–…
–No way! There are only a few clouds in the sky. The forecast is for good weather. You'll see!"

As soon as we arrived at the park, it started to rain. It rained so hard that within five minutes the field was drenched, and so were we. We had no choice but to call it quits and return home. So I spent my Saturday changing channels in search of a baseball game on T.V. My only satisfaction was that Frank wasn't able to go for his swim, either.

The next day, we arranged to meet at the park. But once again, we were out of luck! It was raining cats and dogs. There must be a way to do something about the weather!

The Following Day...

The following day, Ben was desperate. It was STILL raining, with no sunshine in sight. So Ben went to visit his grandmother to ask her advice about the weather. She explained that changes in air pressure affect animals and plants. If Ben were to watch what was happening in nature, he would be able to predict the weather.

Ben wasn't so sure about this, but he told himself that he had nothing to lose. Here are the tricks for predicting the weather his grandmother suggested:

"If a groundhog sees his shadow at noon on Groundhog's Day (February 2), there will be another six weeks of cold weather."

"There's also the old saying: Red sky in the morning, sailors take warning. Red sky at night, sailors' delight."

"Along the coast, people often hang a clump of kelp on their doors. When the weather is warm and dry, the kelp shrivels up and dries out. When the weather turns humid, the kelp absorbs the moisture and takes on its natural form again."

"Then there are the weather cones. When it's dry out, the scales of a pinecone harden, shrink, and open up. When the climate is humid, the scales absorb humidity and soften, and the cone closes up, returning to its natural shape. When it's about to rain, the scales close tightly around the cone."

Just in case his grandmother had left out something, Ben decided to visit the meteorological station in his town. The meteorologists explained several things about the weather. Ben found out that a high pressure zone, called an anticyclone, gradually causes air to descend and heat up with the result that the weather becomes warmer and dryer. In contrast, a low pressure zone causes the air to rise and cool, resulting in the formation of clouds and rain.

Ben was fascinated by the instruments and the technologies used by the meteorologists to predict the weather. He realized that there were ways to plan his baseball games around the weather. All he needed was his own weather station filled with instruments like those he had just seen!

Constructing a Home-Made Weather Station

Do you want to be a meteorologist? Would you like to build your own meteorological station and to be able to measure atmospheric pressure, temperature changes, precipitation, and the speed of the wind?

Thanks to this do-it-yourself weather station, you'll be able to talk knowledgeably about the weather. The weather has an impact on our daily lives. It determines whether we can go on a picnic or play a game of baseball. Weather is a topic that everyone is interested in. For scientists, the study of the weather, called meteorology, is the state of the atmosphere at a given place and a given time. What does the weather mean to you?

Constructing a Water Barometer

We are surrounded by air. You can't often see it, but it is always there. Air is heavy. It weighs down on you and on the earth. This is called atmospheric pressure and it is a good indicator of what kind of weather we are about to receive. Why? Because atmospheric pressure is constantly changing. The higher the pressure, the better the chance of good weather. The lower the pressure, the more the chance of rain.

A barometer is an instrument that measures atmospheric pressure. You can make your own barometer using either water or air by following the directions on this page or on the next one.

Materials required:
- a brick
- a container at least 15 cm in depth
- a pencil
- adhesive tape
- a plastic bottle
- a piece of cardboard
- a strip of paper

Directions:
1. Pour 6 to 7 cm of water into the container. Fill the bottle three-quarters full with water.
2. Place the piece of cardboard over the opening of the bottle to keep the water from flowing out as you turn the bottle and place it in the container. Pull away the cardboard once the bottle is inverted in the container.
3. Attach the brick to the bottom of the bottle with tape so that it doesn't fall over.
4. Tape the strip of paper vertically to the bottle. Mark where the water level is inside the bottle.

With this barometer, if the atmospheric pressure is high, the water will rise in the bottle. If the pressure is low, the level of water will fall.

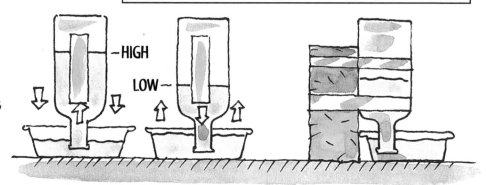

HIGH

LOW

Constructing an Air Barometer

Materials required:
- a balloon
- an elastic band
- a jar
- a straw
- a pin or thumbtack
- a rectangular piece of cardboard, 5 cm taller than the jar
- a pencil
- adhesive tape or glue
- a cardboard right-angle triangle

Directions :
1. Cut the balloon so that you can stretch it over the opening of the jar and secure it with the elastic band.
2. Glue the pin to one end of the straw and glue the other end of the straw to the centre of the balloon.
3. Draw graduated markings on the cardboard rectangle. Glue or tape the triangular cardboard to the rectangular piece so that the rectangle stands upright facing the pin.

If the atmospheric pressure is low, the balloon on the jar will curve outward. If the pressure is high, the balloon will curve in toward the jar.

Now you can consult your barometer every day at the same time. Record the changes in atmospheric pressure as well as what kind of weather you're having.

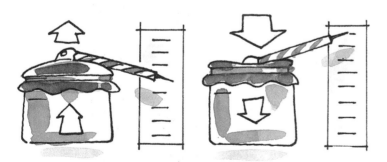

Constructing a Weather Vane

A weather vane (or weather cock) is used for measuring the direction the wind is blowing. Remember that wind is really air in motion. Wind is formed when the sun heats the earth's surface. In turn, the land and the water heat the air above them.

Here's how you can build your own weather vane.

Materials required:
- a sturdy piece of cardboard
- a geometry compass or a circular object
- a stick or broom handle
- a pair of scissors
- a compass
- a hammer
- a nail

Directions :

1. Cut a 25 cm x 50 cm rectangle from the cardboard. Trim one end to make a point and cut a slit into the other end. Cut a second rectangle, 10 cm x 6 cm. Slide this rectangle into the slit and you have your weather vane.

2. Cut a circle (at least 10 cm in diameter) out of the cardboard. Mark on it the directions N-NW-W-SW-S-SE-E-NE, just like on a real compass. Cut a hole in the centre of the compass card slightly larger than the broom handle.

3. Drive the broom handle or stick into the ground. Slide the compass card over the broom handle. Nail your weather vane to the top of the broom handle, being sure to check that it can spin freely.

4. Find north on your real compass and orient your compass card to match it. Tape your card in place so that it won't move around.

Constructing an Anemometer

Here are the directions for building an anemometer that will allow you to measure the speed the wind is blowing.

Materials required:
- a large protractor
- a carpenter's level
- 30 cm of string
- adhesive tape
- a ping pong ball

Directions:
1. Tape one end of the string to the protractor, and the other end to the ping pong ball.
2. Tape the protractor to the carpenter's level.
3. Holding the level so that the bubble of air inside is centred, record the angle shown by the ball when the wind blows against the ball.
4. Use the table below to convert the angle of the ball into kilometres per hour.

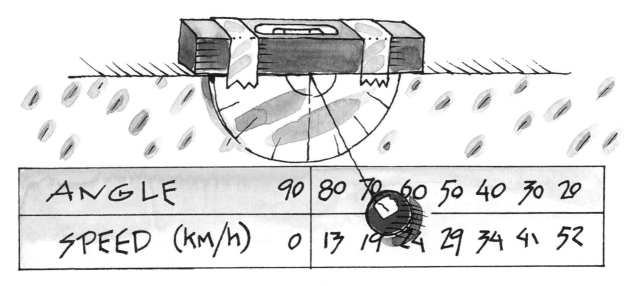

ANGLE	90	80	70	60	50	40	30	20
SPEED (km/h)	0	13	19	24	29	34	41	52

Constructing a Pluviometer or Rain Gauge

A rain gauge (pluviometer) is an instrument which measures the amount of rain or snow that falls to the ground. To be effective, it must be placed in a wind-sheltered spot far from trees or walls. Here is one way to build your own rain gauge.

Materials required:
- water-proof tape
- a permanent marker or pen
- a pair of scissors
- a plastic pop bottle
- a ruler

Directions:
1. Carefully cut off the top of the bottle. Turn it upside-down and place it inside the bottle.
2. Place a strip of tape along one side of the bottle. With the permanent marker, mark the centimetres on the tape, starting from the bottom of the bottle.
3. Place your rain gauge outside in an area away from trees or walls. To keep it from tipping over, surround it with earth.

Constructing a Meteorological Instrument Shelter

Weather instruments are generally placed in an instrument shelter. In this way, they are protected from direct sun and wind. This kind of shelter, sometimes called a Stevenson Screen, is placed on a post one metre above ground level. You will probably need an adult to help you build this.

Materials required:
- 4 wooden legs, each 1 metre long
- 6 wooden panels, each 40 cm x 30 cm
- two hinges and screws
- glue
- a hammer and nails
- a drill
- a screwdriver

Directions: (Remember to have an adult there to help you!)
1. Drill several holes into 4 of the 6 panels.
2. Glue or nail 5 of the panels together to form a box.
3. Screw the hinges to the door and the front of the box.
4. Fix the legs to the base of the box.

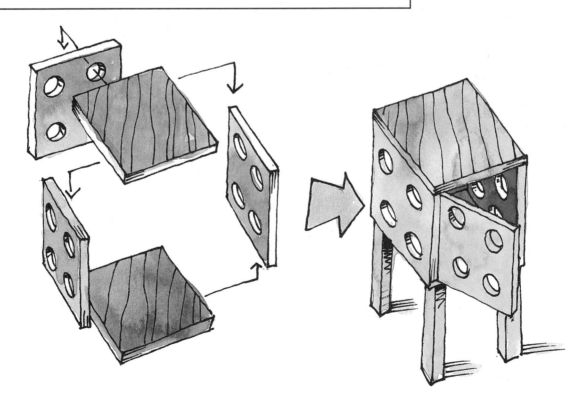

Now you can place your thermometer and barometer inside the instrument shelter. Record the temperature every day. Remember to thank the adult who helped you build this shelter.

The Sun and Wind at Work

Can the forces of the sun and wind
be harnessed to provide sources of energy?

Tales Told by Water

Mousna, Prisoner in a Droplet

My First Visit to the Clouds

Hi. My name is Mousna and I'm a salmon egg. I live among the pebbles on the riverbed with the other roe while I develop. It is usually very calm here, but today the pebbles are moving and spinning about in all directions. What is happening?

I'm no longer in my spawning grounds. Instead, I'm flowing with the current of the river. Luckily for me, my eyes had a chance to develop. Even though I'm still inside my jelly-like egg, I can see where I'm going. Oh no! I'm headed for an enormous waterfall!

Trapped in the falls, I am so afraid that I shut my eyes tightly. I can feel my poor little embryo (that's my body) being hurled against the rocks, bouncing and whirling in all directions. I'm so dizzy! But wait a minute! Now it feels like I'm floating in the air! It's warmer, too. What is going on? I open my eyes cautiously to take a peek.

It can't be! I'm trapped in a droplet of water that has evaporated with the heat from the sun. As I travel toward the sky, I can see the huge waterfall, my river, and the adult salmon making their way up the river to spawn.

Yikes! I'm rising higher and higher all the time! My droplet of water isn't the only one up here. It's as though a meeting of water droplets has been called up in the sky. I have no idea where I am now. When I try to ask, the other droplets simply tell me that we're in a cloud. What's a cloud?

It's getting cooler now and my droplet friends are disappearing, one after the other. I have no idea where they are going, but I have a feeling I'll soon find out. I'm falling back toward the ground!

My Second Journey

I'm cold. The wind is carrying me over an immense forest. I'm getting so dizzy I can't bear to look! Whew! I've landed. It's dark in here and I don't have much room to move. I've filtered my way into the ground and I'm flowing toward an underground stream.

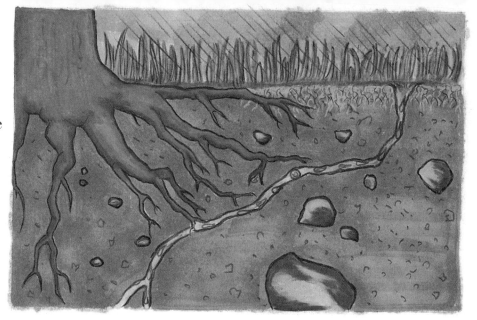

Suddenly I am sucked into a tube. "Where am I now?"

"Welcome to my home. I'm a tree."

Without any effort at all, the tree's capillaries carry me to the top branches.

Resting inside the highest branch, I can feel the tree swaying in the wind. The liquid around me is being warmed with the sun. The tree starts to transpire. This is its way of cooling down. As the tree replaces warm water with cooler liquid (a process called *transpiration*), I can feel myself slipping out of the needles of the tree.

So now I'm drifting through the air again to join my friends for another meeting in the clouds. Today, the wind is stronger and it's colder. The clouds are drifting toward the snow-covered mountains.

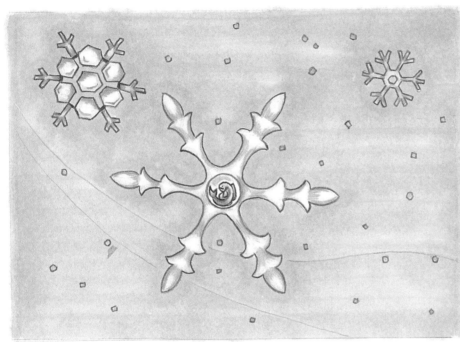

It's freezing out! My droplet friends are cold, too. They're all white and frosty looking. Slowly, I drop down from the sky, twirling and dancing as I go. I guess it's my new shape that makes me fall more slowly. My landing is much more gentle this time. I'm at the peak of a snow-covered mountain, but I can't see around me. Other snowflakes keep landing on top of me, and they're heavy!

I'm not cold anymore, I'm frozen… solid! I can't think when I'm this cold, so I'll take a long nap…

A loud noise awakens me. The ice around me is starting to crack and melt. But it's still so cold that I'm not turning into water, I'm subliming. *Sublimation* is when ice evaporates into the air without first becoming a liquid. While you think about sublimation, I'll think about what's happening to me this time…

39

My Third Voyage

These trips aren't exactly what you would call relaxing. Falling on the ground the first time was brutal. Landing at the summit of a mountain wasn't great either. I thought I would finish my days in an ice cube. On my next trip, I would really like to land in some water!

Hey! I just realized that the bubble I am in has changed from a gas to a liquid. That's called *condensation*, in case you are wondering. When there's enough condensation in the air, then it's back to earth we go, in the form of precipitation.

It's precipitating now! My raindrop is falling and I can see a stream down below. I wonder if I'll be lucky enough to land in it. I'm too scared to look. Plunk! No, I'm not in the water. But I'm not in the ground either. I'm at the surface and the rain water is flowing toward the stream I wanted to land in.

Finally, I'm back in the water again! If only I could grow up quickly and get out of my egg, then my air travels would be over. Here I go, gently flowing with the current.

But as I near a big rock, a wave catches me and sends me in a different direction. My gentle stream hurls itself into a wide river. As I am tossed along, I have no control over my direction. Then I hear the roar of a waterfall, which reminds me of my first trip.

Oh no! Here I go again. But this waterfall is different from the first one. It's a giant pipe. What will happen to me?

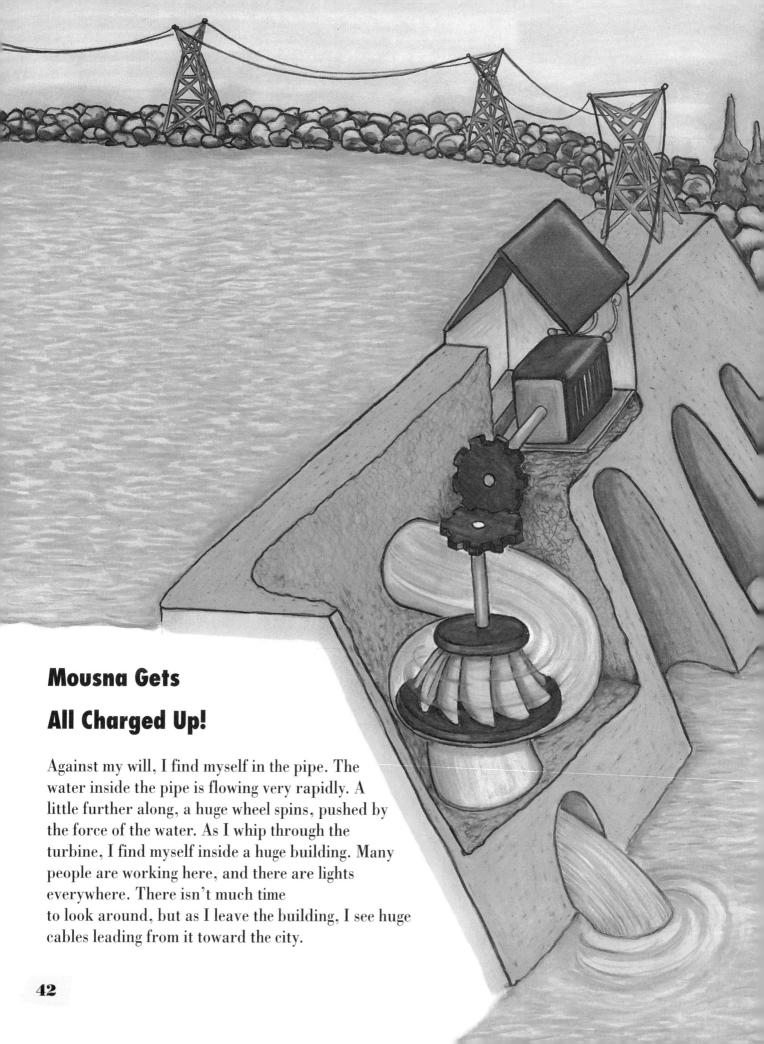

Mousna Gets
All Charged Up!

Against my will, I find myself in the pipe. The
water inside the pipe is flowing very rapidly. A
little further along, a huge wheel spins, pushed by
the force of the water. As I whip through the
turbine, I find myself inside a huge building. Many
people are working here, and there are lights
everywhere. There isn't much time
to look around, but as I leave the building, I see huge
cables leading from it toward the city.

As I continue downstream, I suddenly realize that this is MY river. At last it is calm, so I rest against a rock for a moment. There isn't any room inside my egg now to move. What do I see? Several fry are swimming toward me. I so want to join the tiny fish! In my excitement, I break out of my shell. Finally, I'm free!

I've learned one thing during my adventures. The life of a water droplet is never dull!

Hello, Raindrop! Where Have You Been?

"Hey, Mother Ocean! Can you see me? Here I come!"

"Hello, my little droplet. How are you?" Mother Ocean stretched the crest of a wave just in time to catch her daughter, Raindrop, as she fell from the sky.

"Oh, Mother Ocean, if only you could come with me! You would see so many wonderful things!"

"Unfortunately, Raindrop, that isn't possible. The sun only takes fresh water from my salty body of water. The salt in me is too heavy to evaporate into the air. That's not such a bad thing, either. Imagine what would happen if rain were to contain salt water. People, plants, and animals would no longer have the fresh drinking water that they are used to getting from the lakes and streams."

"Well, then they would just have to drink salt water," answered Raindrop decidedly.

"Think about what you've said, Raindrop. Living things drink water because they're thirsty. Salt water would only make them more thirsty."

Raindrop burst into laughter. "Then, they would drink even more salt water! That would make them thirstier yet, and pretty soon, they would look just like me! Ha! Ha! Imagine if people were pear-shaped. They would find it hard to walk."

"On the contrary, my dear. Living organisms need fresh water to nourish their cells. If they were to drink salt water, the fluid would flow out of their cells, and their bodies would slowly lose all their water."

"What do you mean? How could that happen?"

"The fluid in an organism's cells is a lot like me. It contains salt and other particles. When fresh water circulates through the body, it helps to clean out the cells. Excess salt and particles move from the cells to the fresh water in the veins, thus preventing these waste products from building up too much within the cells. Now, if salt water like me replaced the fresh water, the fluid inside the cells would flow out to dilute the salt water, leaving behind the particles, and the cells would shrink. The cells would no longer function properly."

"That sounds complicated. I shouldn't have laughed before."

"Don't worry, Raindrop. You were just using your imagination. But, tell me, what did you see during your travels?"

I'm kind of thirsty. What about you?

"Oh yes! Well, at first I didn't see anything because the sun had evaporated me into thin air. Once I was high up in the sky, the air started to cool. Then I got my liquid shape back by collecting all my particles."

"That's called condensation."

Raindrop continued her story. "The other raindrops and I gathered together to form a cloud. While floating up there, I could see a family at the beach. The father was boiling water over a campfire. He had forgotten to put on the lid. Inside the pot, all my droplet friends were transformed into vapour and floated up to join us. By the time the father got back to the pot, there was no water left in it and he had to start all over."

"Oh, he'll learn from his mistakes. The next time he'll remember that water evaporates with heat," added Mother Ocean softly.

"I also saw a little girl brushing her teeth. She had poured fresh water into a cup to rinse out her mouth. But instead of emptying her rinse water into the stream, she poured it into a small hole she had dug into the ground. Why would she go to all that trouble?"

"The dirty water will flow through the dirt and gravel. Before it gets back to the stream, it will be clean again. All of the impurities will have been filtered out by the earth."

"So the stream won't become polluted, and you won't fill up with dirty water!"

"Precisely."

"Oh, I almost forgot! The little boy in the family was so excited. He went for a swim in your water, Mother Ocean, and he floated on his back for the first time! His father told him that it was easier to float in salt water than in fresh water. Is that so?"

"Yes, that's right. Salt water is denser than fresh water. It's the salt that makes the difference. The more salt there is, the easier it is for objects to float. Now, my curious little one, you've had enough lessons for today. You should get some rest before the sun rises and takes you off again. Come, I'll rock you to sleep in my waves."

Did You Know That...

...between 100 and 400 litres of water per day may be lost through a dripping faucet?

...watering a lawn takes approximately 1 000 litres of water?

...washing a car with the garden hose can use approximately 300 litres of water?

...a dishwasher uses about 45 litres of water per wash?

...taking a bath requires nearly 160 litres of water?

...taking a shower requires nearly 130 litres of water?

...a family of four living in a Third World country uses only about 15 litres of water per day?

...preparing a meal could use about 18 litres of water?

...washing a single load of laundry uses about 90 litres of water?

...brushing your teeth with the tap turned off while you brush will still use at least a litre of water?

...washing your face in running water could take 7 litres of water?

...water consumption per person in Canada is about 230 litres per day?

...water consumption per person in Third World countries is about 4 litres per day?